the true story of

Stellina

matteo pericoli

Alfred A. Knopf   New York

This is the true story of Stellina.

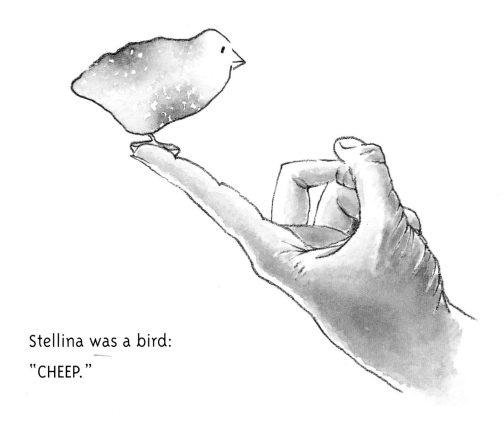

Stellina was a bird:

"CHEEP."

A very little bird:

"CHEEP!"

Holly, my wife,
once saw a very little bird
on the corner of
46th and Third.
In Manhattan.
Cars were rushing by,
ROOOOOAAAAARRRR!
Cars are loud in the city.

But "CHEEP," Holly heard.
Holly, my wife, has very good ears.
Could you also have heard
"CHEEP"
on the corner of
46th and Third,
in the middle of the day,
while cars were rushing by?
ROOOOOAAAAARRRR!
That's not easy to hear.

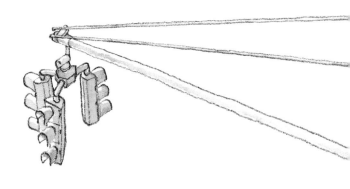

But, as I was saying,
"CHEEP," she heard all of a sudden.
A bird, a very little bird,
had fallen from her nest.

Her nest must have been
(and this is what we think)
inside a traffic-light post.
High, high above
the corner of
46th and Third.

Holly, my wife,
waited and waited.
And waited and waited.
She hoped, she told me,
that the very little bird's mother,
"CHEEP,"
would soon return
to take her home,
back to her nest.

But her mother didn't return.
Who knows why she didn't,
or where she went.

So Stellina,
"CHEEP,"
stood out there for a while,
not knowing what to do,
not knowing what to say
(except, of course:
"CHEEP"),
and not knowing
how to get around,
all by herself,
in such a *b i i i i g* place
as MANHATTAN.

It was evening when Holly, my wife,
decided to take Stellina home with her.

They sat together for a while,
looking at each other,
and both must have wondered:
"And now? What's going to happen now?"

They spent hours and hours together.

From home,
they used to go out
to many places.
They always traveled by subway.
Holly, my wife, carried Stellina in a little box
where she patiently sat
without saying a word.

Perhaps only
"CHEEP" every once in a while.
But nothing else.
Or maybe she was wondering:
"And now? What's going to happen now?"

Stellina would go with Holly, my wife,
to her office,
"CHEEP,"
and stand there,
on her desk,
looking at her.
"CHEEP," she would tell her
every once in a while.

After the office they would leave,
this time to go to the dance studio.
Because Holly, my wife, is a dancer.

So while Holly was dancing—
"Olé!" (she dances Spanish dances)—
Stellina would watch,
"CHEEP,"
and watch,
"CHEEP CHEEP,"
and grow while she looked at Holly.

Stellina was growing because she was eating.

"That's normal!" you would say.

"I am growing because I am eating, too!"

And you are right to say so.

But Stellina was supposed to be fed by her mama
(a bird),

and Holly, my wife, was not her mama
(or a bird).

Little wild birds usually want
only their mothers to feed them,
and they are very picky about it.

They often say, "No one can feed me,
except my mama!"

But Holly, my wife, was patient,
very patient and loving.
She would peel and squeeze fresh grapes
into Stellina's beak,
crumble hard-boiled eggs,
and use her finger, her pinky finger,
to feed Stellina,
who was very hungry,
"CHEEP,"
and who stood there, all the time,
with her beak open wide—
like this: "AAAAAAAHHHH."

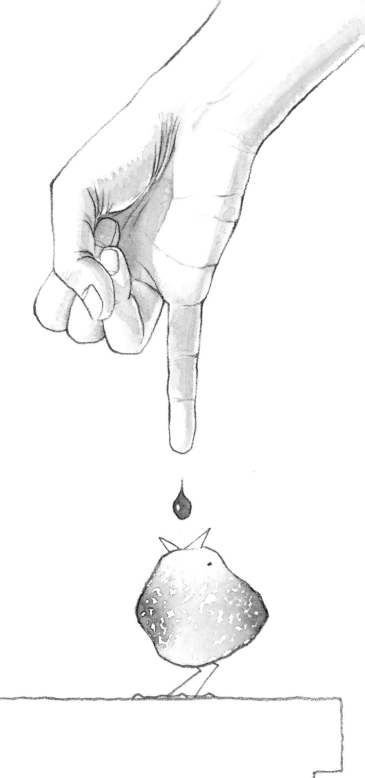

"Why not?"
Stellina must have thought.
"Holly can be my mother for a while."

Stellina started to love Holly, my wife,
probably after their first day together.
And each day more and more.
And Holly, too,
couldn't stop loving Stellina.

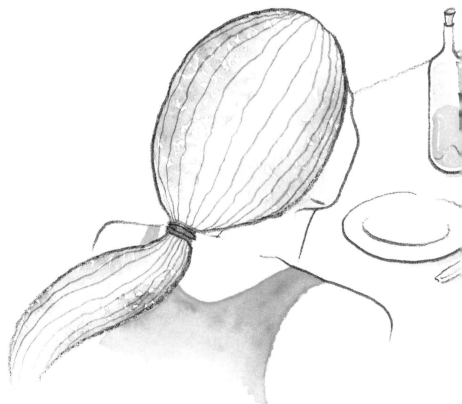

Then, one day,
Stellina learned how to eat by herself,
and Holly was so happy.
She didn't have to feed her
with her pinky finger any longer.
And she didn't have
to watch her all the time.
Or take her wherever she went.
Stellina was growing up.

And then, another day,
Stellina learned how to fly,
all by herself,
and Holly was so excited,
because Holly, my wife,
doesn't know how to fly.
She knows how to dance,
but not how to fly.

So Stellina,
"CHEEP,"
started to fly out of her cage
and around the apartment,
looking for Holly.
She would sit on her head.
Or on her shoulder.
Or on her arm.

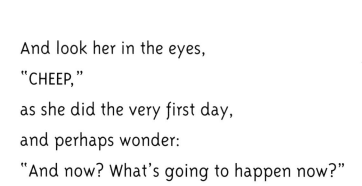

And look her in the eyes,
"CHEEP,"
as she did the very first day,
and perhaps wonder:
"And now? What's going to happen now?"

She sang and flew
and sang and flew around all the time.
Two sounds made her sing
more than any others.

One was the shower,
especially when Holly, my wife,
was taking one.

The other was the sound of the piano.
"CHEEP CHEEP!" she sang along.

Whenever I was drawing at my desk,
she would fly to my head
and play with my hair,
trying to build a nest.
Once she even flew to the pencil
I was holding in my hand.
And stayed there for a while,
bobbing and swaying
and holding on to it tightly.

Stellina lived with us
for a very long time,
in the living room
of our small apartment
in Manhattan.

We left Stellina's cage open
so that she could fly
around the apartment.
But we never let her fly outside,
since she was only used to Holly, my wife,
to me, to her cage,
and to this kind of life.

She often sat on the windowsill
and looked out.
There wasn't that much to see,
except a few windows and a tree.
She looked pensive at the windowsill.
She must have wondered:
"And now? What's going to happen now?"

Every night Stellina would fluff her feathers,
raise one leg, tuck her head into a wing,
and go to sleep.
She lived in a cage,
a cage that was her home,
and she knew it was her home.

We often wondered if her mama,
her birdie mama,
knew where she was.
And also wondered how her life,
so different from other birds' lives,
would have been if Holly, my wife, hadn't heard
"CHEEP" that day, many years ago,
in the middle of the
ROOOAAARing traffic.

She might not have survived that very night,
and she might not have lived to love Holly, my wife.
And she might not have lived to be loved so much
by Holly, my wife, by me, and by everyone else who met her.
But still we wonder.

Her name was Stellina.
She died not long ago
after more than eight years with us,
in our apartment,
not too far from that post where she was born.

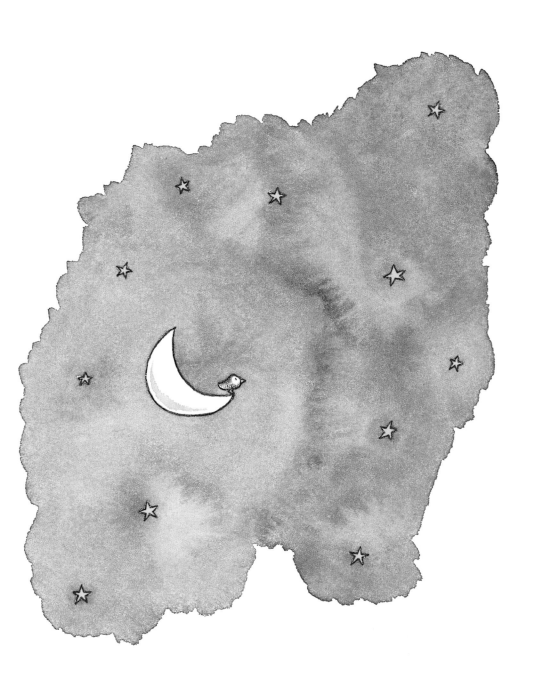

Her name was Stellina,
which, in Italian, means
"little star."

*The author would like to thank
Beverly Horowitz, Melissa Nelson, and Joan Slattery
for their enthusiasm.*

Library of Congress Cataloging-in-Publication Data
Pericoli, Matteo.
The true story of Stellina / Matteo Pericoli.
p. cm.
ISBN 0-375-83273-4 (trade) — ISBN 0-375-93273-9 (lib. bdg.)
1. Wild birds as pets—New York (State)—New York—Biography—Juvenile literature.
2. Pericoli, Matteo—Homes and haunts—New York (State)—New York—Juvenile literature.
3. Pericoli, Holly—Homes and haunts—New York (State)—New York—Juvenile literature.
I. Title.
SF462.5.P47 2006
636.6'862—dc22
2004061503

MANUFACTURED IN MALAYSIA
March 2006
10 9 8 7 6 5 4 3 2 1
First Edition

s t e l l i n a was born in Manhattan in the spring of 1995. Her nest was inside a horizontal pipe holding a traffic light on the corner of Third Avenue and 46th Street. Just a few weeks old and still unable to fly, she prematurely abandoned her nest, for reasons that we don't know. Stellina was rescued by a store security guard, who later gave her to Matteo Pericoli's future wife, Holly, who sat down and waited for the little bird's mother to return. When she realized that Stellina's mother was not coming back to feed her, Holly decided to take Stellina home. She called two New York City zoos, but neither one could take the little bird since she was a common wild finch and not an endangered species. Thus Stellina stayed with Holly, with whom she learned how to eat, sing, and fly, in her apartment on the Upper West Side of Manhattan. When Matteo and Holly moved in together, Stellina came along and lived with them until she died in the late summer of 2003.

m a t t e o p e r i c o l i was born in Milan, Italy, in the summer of 1968. He studied architecture at the Polytechnic School of Milan, and in the winter of 1995 he moved to New York City. After just a few weeks in the city, he met Stellina at his future wife's apartment on the Upper West Side, where Stellina had already learned how to eat, sing, and fly. Since that time, Matteo has been working in New York City as an architect, illustrator, teacher, and author. His books include *Manhattan unfurled* (2001), *Manhattan within* (2003), and *See the City: The Journey of Manhattan unfurled* (2004), his first work for young readers. Matteo and Holly, his wife, live in New York City.

BAKER & TAYLOR